MW01109916

SiR SiLLy

SiR SiLLy

THE WORLD WHERE WORDS PLAY

David Dayan Fisher

© David Dayan Fisher 2013

Published by Sunnyfields Publishing

The right of David Dayan Fisher to be identified as the Author of the Work
has been asserted by him in accordance with the Copyright,
Designs and Patents Act 1988.

All rights reserved. No part of this publication may be reproduced in a
retrieval system or transmitted by any means, electronic or mechanical,
photocopying or otherwise, without the prior permission of the
copyright holders.

Written by David Dayan Fisher (Sir Silly)
Front cover and inside illustrations by Patricia Krebs
Photograph of Sir Silly (back cover) By Emmanuel Todorov
All cover and inside illustrations belong ot the artist, Patricia Krebs
Typesetting by wordzworth.com

ISBN: 978-1-4849-6214-5

SiR SiLLy

is very serious about being silly

Good-bye, hello, welcome, and good night.
Introducing the wonderful world of Sir Silly.
He was born before time, and so he has no time for such time
that was before that time.

He thinks in rhyme and always lets his imagination dance freely.
Sir Silly is all he can be, to be as silly as he can. It seems to have
never left him since he was a little boy.

He plays with words and the pictures that they can create. Some
play with paint, chalk, or pencils. Others are actors and play with
characters and their voices. Then there are those who give us
music, who play with tunes and words together.

It's all about making fun out of having fun and maybe being funny
while doing so. Please enjoy the silly side of a man soaked in silly.

May all that you read
Give you all that you see
And all you that see
Make you read with glee.

Sir Silly is in all of us. I hope you find him in you.

Welcome to the world where words play.
These poems are for children who should never grow up and for
those who never did.

This book is dedicated to the child in all of us, to all the children
I have known, and to all the children who get to know Sir Silly.

About the Author, Sir Silly.

David (Sir Silly) is an actor, an author, an artist, and a poet. From a young age he always wanted to play for a living and never grow up. He plays with characters and his voice in movies and on TV as an actor, with words in poems and stories in books, and with color and texture in his art.

Previous children's books by David Dayan Fisher:
Puppy School
Oakley and the Grump

Dedicated to my mother,
Pebbles, Louie, &
Little Arthur Pearce

thank you to a beautiful friend,
my muse.

Contents

SiR SiLLy's World

There is a world,
A wonderful world,
Where the wonders or words work their way.
Which way they work,
In this wonderful world,
Is the way that Sir Silly plays.
Silliness is in his bones.
He has silly shouts
And silly moans.
The fun of fun,
The games he plays.
The words that twist,
The words he says.
The wonderful world,
Where words work wonders,
Is where Sir Silly spends his days.

The Story of Time That Rhymes

Once upon a time,
The clock struck five past nine.
The hours told the minutes,
It's seconds that makes things fine.
And so the day slept into the night
And the night slept through the day.
The seconds skipped inside the minutes,
As the minutes and hours played.
Tick tock,
The time of the clock.
The seconds of minutes.
It never stops.
Minutes to hours.
Hours to days.
Nights pass so quietly,
So that the morning can play.
Once upon a time,
The clock struck five past nine.
And so it is. And so it was.
The story of time that rhymes.

The Adult and The Child

GROW UP!
No.
I'm small and a child.
I'm meant to be silly and short and wild.
DON'T DO THAT! DO AS YOU'RE TOLD!
What?
Be like you,
Tall, boring, and old?
BEHAVE. BE QUIET.
STOP THAT NOW!
I can't. I'm a child. I don't know how.
Let me be
The size I am.
The age of silly,
With no adult plan.
You were a child.
You were like me.
What happened to you?
You don't seem free.
I'M BIGGER, KNOW MORE.
DO AS YOU'RE TOLD.
I KNOW BEST BECAUSE I AM OLD.
Old is not smarter,
Smart is not big.
You forgot how to be silly,
And that you were once a kid.

In a Faraway Land

In a time that was then
And a land that was far,
When the world was the way it was,
There were many who went
And few that stayed,
But more who didn't, just because.
And so it was.
And so it shall be.
And then it might not be that.
For the time was far
And the land was then.
And they never knew who left the hat.

Tidy your Room

Do as you are told.
Tidy your mess.
Clean your room.
Do the best.
The shouts,
The words
The parents say.
A tidy room
Makes everything OK.
The clothes,
The toys,
The things we enjoy.
The untidy rooms
Of girls and boys.
Put them back.
Find them a home.
The books on the shelf,
The cupboard for the clothes.
The soldiers,
The Barbies,
The Legos,
The cars.
The shoes,
The games,

The candy bars.
Clean them up.
Put them away.
A tidy room
Is fun to play.
A thing has a home,
A home has things,
Like a boot has laces
And a puppet has strings.
The mess was made,
So the tidy can be done.
It's like going backward,
Rewinding the fun.

Music

ROCK AND ROLL
BEEBOP, JIVE.
SOUL AND FUNK,
STAYING ALIVE.
Country, rap,
A heavy metal slap.
A hippie ditty,
A campfire clap.
TUNES OF WORDS,
WORDS OF TUNES.
MUSIC TO DANCE,
SOUNDS TO MOVE.
LYRICS OF LOVE,
MELODIES THAT SING.
Rhythms that flow,
The joys they bring.
Telling us how,
Our listening time.
The wisdom of music
In words that rhyme.

The Dog

I like to sit
And lie around.
I don't need much,
It's true.
Some food,
A treat,
And lots of love,
And a nice juicy bone to chew.

If

If a bubble was in trouble,
Who would save it?
If a lion had a limp,
Who would help?
If an ant could not work out his homework,
Who would help him how to work it out?
If the dog had an itch,
And the cat had a twitch,
Or the bird forgot how to fly.
Oh dear, oh dear.
Oh my, oh my.
So many problems to solve.
If the rabbit forgot how to hop,
If the balloon just would not pop,
If the elephant's trunk was seen to have shrunk,
And the shoe would not get on with the sock.
Oh dear, oh dear.
Who knows why?
What could or should we do?
The solution to the problems,
The lie that could be true.
This and that,
The very fact.

The triangle ate the square.
The table ran.
The plant just sang.
The monkey lost his hair.
Always play
Words and games,
Games of words,
And words we say.
Enjoy it all.
It's all for fun.
Got lunch with a friend.
Have to run.

The Ant and Elefant

The ant was upset.
He sat, and he wept.
An elephant asked,

WHAT'S WRONG?

I'm small. I am small.
I want to be tall.
The world is so big and so long.

DON'T BE SAD.
WIPE UP YOUR TEARS.
I'VE GOT A LONG NOSE
AND BIG FLOPPY EARS.

But you're big.
You're tall.
I just feel like a fool.
It's not easy being
An ant.

BUT I'M CLUMSY AND SLOW.
I CAN'T HIDE. THIS I KNOW.
EVERYONE HEARS ME COMING.
I STEP ON TWIGS.
I CRUSH THE BRUSH.
IT'S NOT EASY BEING THE SIZE OF A BUS.
IF I WERE SMALL AND YOU WERE TALL,
THINK OF THE THINGS WE COULD DO.

The ant just sat. He had a think.
The elephant's mind began to blink.
They imagined being each other.

My, oh my!
How much I would eat!
It's heavy work being in an elephant's feet.

AND WHAT A PACE, SO VERY BUSY.
BEING AN ANT WOULD MAKE ME VERY DIZZY.

The ant looked up.
He had a smile.

I think I will stay who I am for a while!

Greedy Dan

There was a greedy old man
Whose name was Dan.
A miserable, wanting, needing man.
He chose the path,
To be ill to his past,
To steal and cheat
And money grasp.
His final years,
His winter life,
He stole from his family
And his poor dead wife.
Greedy, sad,
Fading away,
His health failing,
Greed ate him each day.
And so it was,
A legacy of theft.
Old, sad Dan
Had nobody left.
Money in mind
And very unkind,
He broke his promises
And lost his mind.

They all whispered and knew
The awful truth,
That Old Dan lied.
They had written proof.
To be ill to the past,
To be greedy and take.
His poor dead wife
Just turns in her grave.
But the story is,
And the story shows,
Greedy people
Are sad to the bone.

The Boy Who Called Everyone Stupid

You stupid fool.
You stupid man.
Your team is stupid.
You're a stupid fan.
He called them all,
The short and tall,
The simple and smart.
So very cruel.
Stupid people everywhere.
Stupid clothes
And stupid hair.
The boy who told,
Who was stupidly bold,
Got his stupid justice,
Was in jail till he was old.

Who is stupid now?

Fat Cat

THERE WAS A CAT WHO WAS VERY FAT.
THE MICE THOUGHT IT FUNNY,
AND THEY LAUGHED AT THAT.
They danced around,
They teased, and they squeaked.
The poor fat cat
Was ever so weak.
Meow, meow.
I'm old, and I'm fat.
But if it makes you happy,
I'm a happy cat.

The Croc That Eats Bad Kids

The crocodile
With big white teeth
Loves the taste of children's feet.
He snaps and chews
And nibbles and bites.
He has toes for dinner every night.
An ankle for lunch.
A heel for tea.
He will sometimes feast right up to the knee.
Yellow eyes see all around,
Left and right,
And up and down.
But if you are good,
He will swim right by.

It is the taste of naughty
That makes his hunger cry.
Naughty kids,
Beware of the croc.
He eats bad and mischievous
In his breakfast pot.
Chew, munch,
Gobble, and crunch.
Bad boy Billy he ate for lunch.
Naughty boys and naughty girls,
The croc, he knows your game.
For the story of the croc who eats bad kids
Is the story of crocodile fame.

My Pal Billy

He's crazy mad,
Silly insane.
I think he lost a piece of his brain.
He's nuts,
Bananas,
Gone 'round the bend.
No sense left
In my nutty friend.
His words are muddled,
His clothes inside out.
He whispers for talking
And sneezes shouts.
His shoes are odd,
His socks are too.
From ear to ear,
You can see right through.
The silly side,
His side of silly,
The madness of crazy,
That is my pal Billy.

Scruffles Mcfluffles

Scruffles McFluffles was his name,
With a scruffy chin
And a scruffy mane.
A scruffy face.
A scruffy way.
Scruffles McFluffles
Had scruffy days.
With scruffy, fluffy,
Scruffy words.
And a scruffy walk to match.
Scruffles McFluffles
Was so scruffy,
He would always itch and scratch.

Animals and a Hat

A dog,
A cat,
A frog,
A hat.
One barked,
One cried,
One croaked,
One sat.
A sitting hat,
A crying cat,
A croaking frog,
A barking dog.
Woof,
Croak,
Meow,ww
Sat.
There is no sound
To a sitting hat.

Hopscotch

The frog did hop.
The hop did scotch.
The Scotsman looked at his pocket watch.
The watch chimed nine.
The time seemed fine.
A fine time for a slice of cake
And raspberry wine.
Tea for two,
And two for tea.
The frog and the Scotsman,
And you and me.
Jump in a puddle,
A puddle of fun.
The police chased the robber who was on the run.
Words that rhyme.
The clock that chimed.
A hopping frog.
The Scottish Time.
That's the end,
Or so it seems.
It's breakfast for dinner,
And lunch for ice cream.

Lazy Day

Under the shade of a tree,
I sit in silence, with my dogs beside me.
The sound of the bees
And the birds in the trees.
The peace of nothing, all around me.
The green of it all, from the short to the tall.
The lush grass blanket,
The branched out oak,
The bushes that cover the hills like a cloak.
Quiet with the noise of nature,
The sounds of natural life.
Under a tree in the park with my dogs
Is a wonderful hour away from the wife.

Being a Child

Being silly,
Having fun,
Making noise,
My farting bum.
Dancing,
Skipping,
Being a child.
Imagination running wild.

The Way to Be

Be nice.
Do good.
Treat others the same.
No need for hurt
Or calling names.
To give is a gift,
To help so kind.
To always be in a positive mind.

The Dog and the Cat

The dog and the cat, one day they just sat.
They thought about bones and mice,
This and that.
Then the dog had a game he wanted to play,
But the cat disagreed in every which way.
No, not that!
Said the worried cat.
The dog just smiled
As his mind went wild,
And his growl began to rise.
The cat looked up
As the dog looked down,
With the terror of the game in its eyes.
And so it was.
And so it is.
The game dogs and cats always play.
The idea of the dog,
Which the cat did not like,
The story why dogs chase cats away.

The Cow Said Meow

Meow, said the cow.
No, not like that!
Explained a slightly angry cat.
You got it wrong.
That's my song.
A cow goes moo
And chews grass all day long.
Moo?
Said the cow.
But I don't know how.
Meow seems like fun,
Right here and now.
I'M A CAT!
I SPEAK LIKE THAT!
Does a cowboy wear a soldier's hat?
The cow looked down
As the cat did frown.
He did not like the cow speaking his sound.
Moo, moo.
The cow goes moo.
Everyone knows the tune of you.
The cow had a think.
As the cat's patience did sink,
The cow turned around and gave me a wink.
So I go moo.
You go meow?

YES!
Said the cat.
You've got it now.
The cow shook his head.
I like meow instead.
The cat got so angry
His head went red.
You can't.
It's wrong.
You're singing my song.
Wrong?
Said the cow.
But I don't know how.
JUST SAY IT AND DO IT.
IT'S THE WAY OF THE COW.
Moo, meow.
A cat or a cow.
Is it a law that's written, the rule of how?
I'm just being silly. I'm having a joke.
The cat was so upset
He nearly choked.
The cow laughed.
He forgot to meow.
Moo, moo, moo.
The joke's on you now.

Things

Bananas.
Pears.
Apples and chairs.
Monkeys, dogs, and cats.
Chocolate, cake.
A foggy lake.
What do you think of that?
Cabbage and fun.
Bubblegum.
The horse ran over the moon.
The dog and cat,
They danced to that,
As ice cream ate the spoon.
The pig did bark.
The ant just laughed.
The rabbit read the news.
The loaf of bread
Was known to have said,
It's hard to tie one's shoes.
The land was green.
The cow was sheep.
The policeman stood
As he went to sleep.
The dream of things.
The things of dreams.
The endless ever

Of ever being.
Make it fun.
Always play.
The words I write
From day to day.
Cake, candy,
Giants, and dwarfs.
Buttered stones
And magical horse.
Soldiers eat flowers.
The minutes count hours.
The seconds dance through the day.
The coats of snails.
The bucket of pails.
The wonder of words that play.
Fun to have.
Having fun.
My game of this.
A song of one.
One of me.
Me of three.
Four and five and six.
The poem I wrote,
With a musical note,
From a bag of magical tricks.

Poems

Poems are words that rhyme and match,
Like eggs and legs.
How about that?
A poem has rhythm and dances in tunes,
Said the cat to the dog,
The ice cream to the spoon.
A poem trips,
And flips,
And hops.
It skips,
And jumps,
And belly flops.
Words that join
And sing a song.
Some are short,
And some are long.
The silly play that words can do.
The ones I make,
Especially for you.

So.
Diddly doo,
Diddly dee.
The frog had lunch with a bumblebee.
The ant was king,
The lion a clown.
The monkey and elephant
Jumped up and down.
So a poem it is.
A poem of fun.
Is that the time?
I have to run.

Mysteries of Myths

Ear of elephants,
Elephants' ears,
Footprints of giants,
And reindeers' tears.
Elves' hats,
Talking rats,
Magical bunnies,
And barking cats.
The wonders of stories,
The stories of old.
The tales of myths,
The kings so bold.
The princesses cry.
The hero who flies.
The dragon fire.
The all-seeing eye.

The nasty evil.
The good and the true.
The fantastic stories.
The cow and the moon.
Imagination.
Pictures and words.
Creations of lives,
Real and absurd.

Misplaced Child

An adult is a child who misplaced his way,
Who found his serious and lost his play.
They read the news, moan about work.
They sit in traffic and iron their shirts.
The adult stops the child from play,
As the child does nothing but keep his way.
The silliness of growing up for sure.
The happy child or the adult bore?

The Body

BING BOING,
SPRING AND BOUNCE.
HOP, SKIP, JUMP,
AND POUNCE.
WALK,
JOG, RUN, AND SPRINT.
LOOK,
FROWN,
SMILE, AND WINK.
THROW, CATCH,
PUSH, AND SHOVE.
HANDLE,
TICKLE,
FINGERS IN GLOVES.
DANCE AND SING,
ROLL AND SWING,
JIGGLE AND WIGGLE,
SO MANY THINGS.
THE BODY PLAYS
IN SO MANY WAYS.
WHAT WILL YOURS DO TODAY?

Words

Words.
What a load of silliness.
Bubbles.
Troubles.
Elephants' trunks.
The moon lit the night.
The sun drenched my lunch.
The hippo did dance.
The aardvark laughed.
The rhino sang opera.
The fish had a bath.
The itch lived on.
The sigh shouted out.
The boy in the windmill
Never had a doubt.
Dum dee doo,
Doo dee dum,
The apple and pear
Had tea with the plum.
The cake was fine,
And so was the wine.

They laughed
And giggled
And turned into fruit pie.
Such wonders of wonders,
Such fiddledy sticks.
The nose of the dog
Who does neat tricks.
Circles, squares, cuddly bears.
Peas, cabbage, and tarts.
The silliness of simple words.
The simple, silly art.

To Be or Not To Be?

To be or not to be?
Two, three, five, or six?
To give a get.
To have a not.
To eat the chew of licks.
The foot of hand.
The fingers of toes.
The place of lost.
The way not known.
Inside out.
The muted shout.
The man of child.
The thin and stout.
Go away to here quite quick.
The slow that runs.
The glue unsticks.
The mindless wizard.
The snowless blizzard.
The raincloud full of sun.
What's the how?
When's the then?
The misery of fun.
Do the don't.
The open closed.
The big that's small,

The stop that goes.
Up and down.
Round and round.
The silent words.
The search that's found.
The other way.
The silly sane.
The smart of dumb.
All words of fun.
No idea of wisdom lost.
I write the speech.
The summer frost.
It's all a game.
The unknown fame,
The dog of cats.
The shoe of hats.
Words I write.
The morning night,
I end this song.
The dark and bright.

COME DOWNSTAIRS. YOUR DINNER'S GETTING COLD.

Many Things

There are many things I like to see.
A monkey swinging in the tree.
A lion lying in the sun.
A caterpillar having fun.
A cat with a scratch.
A dog with an itch.
An ant acrobatic that love to flip.
A zebra that sings.
A rat that claps.
A mouse that runs around the traps.

The many things I like to see,
Like the edible dance of the honeybees.
The butterfly.
The crow in the sky.
The rabbits that jump.
The hippos so plump.
The wolves that dance into the night.
That gives the sheep an awful fright.
The cow that moos.
The chicken that grooves.
The chimpanzee's cousin, the great baboon.
The bird of prey.

The praying cat.
The dancing bear.
The spider's map.
The web of life.
The woof of bark.
The meow of kittens in the dark.
The wonders of the other world.
The animals that dance and sing and twirl.
The many things I like to see.
I have to go now.
It's time for tea.

Time

There was a time when there was no time.
Not half past three
Or ten past nine.
The tick didn't tock,
And there were no clocks.
No seconds,
Or minutes,
Or hours to watch.
No lunch,
No tea,
No dinner time set.
No early, no late,
No time to fret.
The trees, the birds, the wolves, the sheep.
The flowers and ants knew when to sleep.
The sun did rise and always fall.
No need for time,
Our scheduled wall.

When was then and nothing else.
The day was the day,
All moments of wealth.
When asked what time, when, and how?
The animals would say,
"Well, it is right now!"

Made in United States
Orlando, FL
23 March 2025

59744741R00031